Victoria Field

The Lost Boys

First published in 2013
by Waterloo Press (Hove)
95 Wick Hall
Furze Hill
Hove BN3 1NG

Printed in Palatino 10.7pt by
One Digital
54 Hollingdean Road
East Sussex BN2 4AA

A CIP record for this book is available
from the British Library

ISBN 978-1-906742-61-4

Acknowledgements

Most of these poems have been previously published, some in earlier versions. I would like to thank the editors of the following anthologies and magazines: *Acumen, Artemis, Great Trees of Cornwall, HQ Magazine, October Guests, Orbis, Peninsula Magazine, Poetry Cornwall, Poetry Ireland Review, Poetry on the Lake Journal, Quadrant, Scintilla, Scryfa, Stone.*

'The Things They Said' was commissioned by Truro Cathedral and broadcast on BBC Radio 4, Sunday Worship in January 2007.

'Wood, String, Air' appeared in The Playing Place, a shipping-container exhibition in Truro, Cornwall, part of the Cornwall Design Season in 2011. The poem became a poster, designed by Daniel Oparison.

'Litany for the Animals' was published on the Quaker Concern for Animals website for St Francis Day 2012.

Thanks to Pol Hodge for the Kernewek in 'Tree of Doors'.

Some of these poems have won prizes, or been commended, or shortlisted in the following competitions: Age Concern, Great Trees of Cornwall, Mirehouse, Poetry on the Lake Short Poem Competition, Silver Wyvern, Strokestown International, Torbay Poetry Competition.

I am grateful for a Hawthornden Fellowship in 2012.

By the same author

Poetry
October Guests with Caroline Carver, Penelope Shuttle
(fal, 2009)
Many Waters – Poems from Ten Months at Truro Cathedral
(fal, 2006)
Olga's Dreams (fal, 2004)

For children
The Gift (fal in association with Truro Cathedral,
December 2007)

Non-fiction
Writing Routes: A Resource Handbook of Therapeutic Writing
edited by Gillie Bolton, Victoria Field, Kate Thompson.
(Jessica Kingsley Publishers, 2010)
Prompted to Write, edited by Zeeba Ansari and Victoria
Field, (fal, 2007)
*Writing Works: A Resource Handbook for Therapeutic Writing
Workshops and Activities* edited by Gillie Bolton, Victoria
Field, Kate Thompson. (Jessica Kingsley Publishers, 2006)

Translation
Giacomo Ponti by Dato Magradze, translation Natalia Bukia
Peters & Victoria Field, (fal, 2012)

Contents

In memory of Monte James Banfield

The Lost Boys

Moonface

As I stir a pan of white sauce
the face of the moon stares back,

skin puckering, craters lifting
and sinking, revealing black beneath.

Suddenly she's beside me, the ghost
of the daughter I never had, standing

on a stool, because she's still small,
my hand covering hers as we push

the spoon through its orbit. Her ivory
skin gleams against dark hair.

Her features are far away and elude me.
Behind us, in the dim kitchen,

her many brothers watch us —
all those boys I never bore,

arrayed in constellations,
numerous and strange as stars.

Finding Myself in the Garden

The leafless honeysuckle gives the finger to the grey sky
black seeds like beads on an old woman's jet necklace

monbretia's sword-like leaves cut what's left of the light with bitterness
orange flowers grasping the air

a mop of bizzie lizzie, pink in an old metal watering can,
still loves romance and is going strong

rosemary's nodding off — her blue-sprigged spring
long since gone

someone's emptied the grow-bags, carted away blighted tomatoes
they wait in a patient line of plastic, eye sockets staring

geraniums never took this year, all came up blind
except the white one — her plentiful flowers stained with liver spots
and rust

the little spruce brought indoors each Christmas
has bright new growth, bless
fuzzy little mittens of needles at the end of every branch

lavender never gives up — got to admire her spirit
opening her heart to any late bee that's passing

last winter cracked some pots, they're still not replaced
dandelion and couch grass ribbon the paving slabs

they say the asiatic lily was magnificent last summer
someone remembers the bright unfurling of mottled nakedness
white and unyielding — dark leaves say nothing

and there's *Fascination* of course, that red rose
incongruous in full bloom — the decade-old wedding present
refusing point-blank to die

and three pots where I planted some seeds from the handkerchief tree
no weeping there, no ghosts and no life that I can see.

Lostwithiel

Willows never forget how it feels
to be young.
> William Stafford

A single rowing boat moves slowly through
the silted shallows of a river once welcoming
ships of the world. Your name was a byword for tin
and abundance — now the guidebook calls you

'much decayed', a place for walking old dogs,
antique shops and early closing. How
does it feel when history has harvested
the best of you — to be a basket of memories

too long for the living? All around, willows bend,
graceful in their sleepy fullness. Lazy ripples
fade away. Nothing is ever as it was —
these passing ghosts, my sad, reflected face

in stilling waters and, on my fingers,
the unexpected tang of salt.

Winter, Mylor

The world is so grey
and so sad. Sometimes,
the tree weeps whole rivers
grieving for her lost leaves.

The Things They Said

The first star said,
I'm a spark adrift
in the sea of night.

The second,
I burn with an icy light.

The third star said,
I'm an arrow pointing the way,
follow me, follow me into the day.

The gold declaimed,
I'm worth less
than the flowers in the field.

The frankincense whispered,
wash me away with the hair of a girl.
When I'm gone, I'm revealed.

The myrrh asked,
I'm beloved and bitter. It's a birth,
but has somebody died?

Said the gifts,
you must give us,
in our going, we'll arrive.

The old king cried,
I need armies, chief priests and power.
My hunger is hate and my anger is fear.

The new king replied …
nothing.
He's asleep in the manger that's also a bier.

The love said,
I'll hurt you, one day I'll go.
That moment's forever with each rising sun.

Say the people, you're crazy.
Say the wise men, we know,
but that night for a moment
stars and earth became one.

Porch

after R.S. Thomas

How close do you feel to God?
asks the priest. As I sit with my back
to the altar, God answers for me,
throws open the locked door

of my heart, turns the heavy ring
of the handle, lifts the stiff catch,
takes away my breath on the swing
of smooth hinges, lets in the air

that is everywhere. God isn't arriving
nor leaving, through this four-chambered
porch under my ribs. He is the opening
and the door, the push and pulse

of whatever moves through me,
the whole red messiness of love.

A Haunting

St Marys, Isles of Scilly

The high bracken is full of spirits. Its prehistoric
scent takes me home to childhood in Kent,
blackberrying, beating back the sap-filled stems

to reach brambles no one else can be bothered with,
fearing, and longing to see, the deft flick of an adder.
The spirits of that village are here now,

clear as day in the island light that's half sky,
half water, Nanny, old Nunc, Mrs Noakes
and Mr Palmer, Mr and Mrs Monk, those girls —

Michelle and Maureen, none living now,
(not as the mainland understands living), but present
in these dense acres of green where I'm lost,

surrounded by sea, not knowing
where I'm going, nor quite where I've been.

From This Height

after Tony Hoagland

of my second floor bedroom
window, I confront the clock
on the church, its round face,
every morning on my waking
every night at my sleeping.

No, I don't deserve the pleasure
of this simple rented house
overlooking wren-filled
sycamores, the wide harbour
with its castles and busy boats.

Nor do I deserve the pain
of this loneliness, evening
to dawn, light slipping in,
creeping over supple sea,
drawn by the sun's slow clock.

Every day, as I climb the hill
behind my house, up granite
steps, over the old cemetery
where history's bodies lie
lost and unmarked, I commit

an act of forgetting, let
the morning take me anew,
let the world grow around
me as the church clock chimes
its first hour of the day, below.

Changing Lives

When Simon dresses as Claire, he
puts on more than a skirt. He wraps
his hardened heart in lace, makes memories
sparkle like jewels and squashes

his burliness under his bra. His longings
teeter on heels and his voice grows girlish
as his gusset. When he tosses his curls,
it seems the whole world dangles

in the tinkle of his laughter and brightness
falls from the summer air to light up his eyes.
As it did that special day, never to be talked of since,

when he and the eminent High Court Judge,
passing as Julie, walked over Perranporth,
kicking the sand, hand in nail-varnished hand.

January, Swanpool

Surfers, tadpole-black and slick,
slide towards land on freezing sea.

Free as fish, they tumble, at one with the water,
while I slip and stumble on the icy path,

tentative, like the silver light
frilling the scallop-edged waves.

I Go Back to May 1997

for DM Thomas

Racing over Beeny Cliff,
pulling wild garlic
on the coast path to Polperro,

I didn't know you were giving me,
a girl with no home town,
the gift of Cornwall.

My suitcases full of clothes
hand-made and formal
from my life in Lahore,

I didn't know I'd never
wear them here, how soon
they'd all be given away.

I didn't know till today
how my life would pivot on
those two weeks that long-gone May —

how some things would fade,
others would flower,
how love, like the tides,
would leave and always return.

Dead Beech Tree at Trebah

All my days these days are blind days, the moon's
face, blank and white, looks in from time to time,

doesn't say a word, so I don't hear her come
and don't hear her go. Night and day are all

the same shade of grey in this country
of the dead. Winters never end in the garden

where everyone's blind, standing stock-still
on our shallow roots each side of the valley,

aching for spring. None of us speak though
we hear signs of life, voices of people and birds,

distant hum of boats and planes, wind
stroking the leaves. They tell me I'm naked

but how would I know, with no limbs left to wrap
round my trunk to test the touch of my skin or feel

for the moss-covered heartbeat of the tree
they can't name or to prise loose chunks of bark

from the Monterey pine, let them fall heavy as slate,
cold as old armour from tanks rumbling down

the rapidly-poured concreted track, nor can I shake
a rich head of hair like the evergreen willow,

nothing moves in me now. No sap rises, no leaves fall,
no swinging branch to lift then drop a child down

to where things might go better, as we wanted them
to in 1944. Then, sunshine pulled desire

up from my roots, my leaves quivered and rose.
Girls of Cornwall bloomed all around, opened

to the young oaks of soldiers so full of promise,
responding with beauty, their thighs pink and silken

as spring magnolias, they flounced lip-sticked and frilled,
filled with the red lust of sudden rhododendrons,

whole minefields of blonde daffodil heads
on the slopes of these gardens, everything flourishing

until those goodbyes when hundreds of handkerchiefs
from a tree full of ghosts dropped sodden into the grass.

One uniformed man, tall as a pine, looking both ways
like an ash tree in March, was mindful of memory.

He scarred me with his pocket knife — sap bleeding
through the date he wanted none to forget — gouging

my skin, sharing the pain of being here now, then,
a year soon only trees will remember, before running

from the enclosed garden of innocence, down to the sea
crossing to another world, one of lolling heads,

heavy as araucaria seeds, shrapnel sharp
as monkey puzzle leaves, the squelch of bodies

soft and open as toads in bamboo, tight knuckled
as bone on old branches and beyond, furnaces

where people burn easy as seasoned wood,
jungles where, like the sudden death of a million

healthy oaks, men fall under the blows of those
who love cherry blossom. I don't need to be told

not to sow for three days in the last days of March.
I'm limbless, silent, scarred, dead from the neck up.

All my days are blind days. I can't see the sun nor feel
on my branches the blood red of a passing robin's breast.

[*Note:* Trebah is a sub-tropical garden in Cornwall, situated on the Helford estuary. On 1st June 1944, a regiment of 7,500 men of the 29 US Infantry Division embarked from Trebah Beach for the D-Day assault on Omaha Beach in Normandy, where they suffered grievous casualties.]

After the Wedding

Everywhere was Sunday-silent by the river in the early morning
as they slid towards me — twenty seven swans describing a heart,

each following the folded cup of the wings of the swan in front,
making a shape that's round, like valleys and hills, breasts and roses,

smiles and eyes, then coming to an apex, like prayer and churches,
like an act of love, spears of irises bright and sharp in the water,

each yellow beak leading, each long neck forward and yearning,
each pair of paddling feet, blessing the river, coming together

like a congregation witnessing love, honouring a rose-crowned bride,
a groom, sheltering as an oak, complete and endless as a pair of gold rings.

Penzance

Only one table's taken in the Exchange Café.
Three women with angular hair talk about Art.

Outside, the town's cold and murky, granite-grey.
Inside this temple of sheet glass,

all is warm and precise, my circular table
shines like a black moon, its craters botoxed.

I read the signs along the small street
retreating from this shock of the new:

Maritas Hair and Beauty has both *Ladies Salon*
and a *Gents*, the Cycle Centre *Stocks Bikes*

For All Ages. A glossy waiter serves me
inky coffee, milk in a white jug, luminous,

Morandi-perfect. The café outside offers handwritten
Breakfast's in various combinations. Here, in all

this air and space I'm hungry for something.
The waiter smiles his bright smile and brings,

without my asking, in not quite a spoon,
not quite a dish, beautifully ambiguous,

(those women would know what to call it)
chocolate beans that melt, bitter and sweet on my tongue.

String

She makes knots
only sailors know

knits regrets
into stout socks
for fishermen

connects his front
to her back
to his top

winds herself into a ball
hides in the hull
of his favourite boat

sings her long thin songs
waits to be needed.

St Davids

From inside the tent, rain sounds loud and when the zip's
unzipped in the morning, dew sings on the feet
away from the retreat centre, where indoor faces are cautious,

unslapped by cold, hands pouring tea for one another from teapots
needing two hands and the peed-on grass steams like the tea,
sea's joining the rain, dew's coming up to the rain like beads that,

if they were beads, are reckless in their spilling all over
this tussocky cliff top — so much wet needs to be wetter —
gulls cry for it, bits of soil and seed from somewhere stick to the feet,

cold, pressed against a warm wall of flesh in the sleeping bag,
a chrysalis waiting for morning to be really morning, the hiss
of the little stove, the little pan, tea bags, plastic mugs,

how such wetness is sweetness, all around on the cliffs
are small brown birds in the bracken, curled for spring
like a bride's hair might be, if she were that kind of bride,

birds whose names are lost in brownness and smallness
but might answer to pipit as gulls answer to wet wind and yearning
to crawl back into the tent, for warmth, to feel skin as thin

as nylon between warm and cold and to cry out because the field
is empty, the sea eats sound, the people in the distance are behind glass,
not drowning in wind and air — inside the tent, under the earth

springs make their journey from deep places as the moon pulses
the sea, while saints and morning birth themselves
again and again and again in all this blessed wetness.

The Dead

The New Year's here.
So many people I loved are not,
and neither is the me I used to be.
I miss us all.

Flight

On the plane, I'm fascinated by the back
of his neck, the way it folds itself like
dough down and around his collar,
how constellations of freckles are bears
and maidens, Pleiades and Pole stars
on the clear sky of his skin, how
a sprinkle of stubbly hair connecting ear
to complicated ear, glints gold against
the white dome of his head, that library
where he keeps his life, where words
from the book he's reading file themselves,
busy and silent in this vastness of sky.

Questions for Vera

What do you keep in that smallest box?

It's where I've locked away my land,
black bread, cabbages and hens,
dots of dandelions in swathes of grass
around our *dacha*, my medals,
the Soviet flag, a *samovar* and glasses,
summer, plunging in cold rivers, my mother.

And in the next?

Here, I've wrapped my losses, the siege
of Stalingrad, the hush of black marias,
like ravens in the snow, hungry cries
of children, empty shelves and secrets,
the camp that took away my lover,
all the disappeared, the ice and lies and blood.

This is the last, the biggest, all six sides
opaque, letting in and out the light, metal
slightly warped, hinge becoming worn …

it's full of the endless days of now,
the television's drone, my tongue that's useless
in this life so far from home, the spent century,
my untouched ageing self, the son who'll never grow …

I slot the other boxes in it, like a *matryoshka* doll
but, still, it's empty, look.
What do you want to know?

Opening the Gate

In five years, we had just two, true conversations.
The first expansive, outside in sunshine, marriage

on both our minds. We were wedding guests
on a perfect May day, everyone joyful, dressed up,

bubbling with mild hysteria. You acknowledged
a wistfulness, too, for those of us not, or not yet,

(and, now, never can be), happily spliced.
At least that's what I read between your easy banter

and serious discussion of churches and religion, like me,
you seemed on the edge, half in half out

but yearning too, wanting to know more about
that one-way gate, the jewelled road tumbling towards

an amazing light and open arms. The second time
we talked one-to-one, was in winter, a cold, dead day

between Christmas and New Year. Kind friends
brightened the darkness with a party and games

but you, subdued, were not quite there,
told me it had been a dreadful year.

More and more, you said, you'd been in the cathedral
asking the questions it understands so well

but finding no answers. 'A permanent solution
to a temporary problem,' someone said, afterwards,

not seeing the solution's already a given,
the dilemma's not why, but how, what and when,

the why-nots of love, work and friends, irrelevant,
they'll all soon be gone, in any case. Not a moment of madness,

you choreographed a small theatre of action, and then?
Was it a drop through cool dark to a nothingness of total peace?

Or did you spiral skyward past blossom and birds
to the embrace of a bride, and the blue of her miraculous eyes?

St Clether Holy Well

... the little words that come
out of the silence, like prayers
                          Wendell Berry

pink says the foxglove, going to seed
brown the dying bracken
grey murmurs the spreading lace of lichen

stone and *grass* says the path
come, go, step, gate

trees repeat over and over
leaf, leaf, leaf, leaf

the well's words are ancient —
earth
deep
clear
once

and the chapel's too —
roof, walls
altar, dark

three flickering candles keep their counsel
each proclaiming their one small word

light

Banting House Inn

David finds me a second blanket
makes sure the washroom's pristine.
Paul thinks London is cool, offers
to show me toronto.com,
has the computer switched on 24/7.
Brandon poaches eggs with a timer,
serves them sprinkled with parsley,
a crescent of melon. James carries
heavy cases up two flights of stairs, turns
his grimace to a smile that reaches his eyes.

All day, they fold towels, dust the many
clocks, their shorts and piercings at odds
with polished wood and the wall-papers'
many varieties of floral, in this house
of Dr Banting, discoverer of insulin,
testing its effect on himself, being,
like James, Brandon, Paul and David,
a man concerned first for the comfort of others.

The Lost Boys

The theatre's full of the hard-to-hear chatter
of lost boys describing
toys no one will buy them for Christmas

Some boys get lost when they are so little
no one's yet pinned a name on them —
they disappear in the hot flame

of a hospital furnace
along with bandages, diseased kidneys
love-filled blood from their mother

Some have names but never know them
warm, well-fed and teddied
they drift away to wherever it is they want to go —

forget to wake up. Childhood's a big country —
boys want to map it as soon as they can —
toddling towards the sheen of a deep pool

pointing a cocked gun at their brother in fun
Some boys lose themselves from the inside out —
once strong bones eaten by ice

Boys who think they know where they're going
on the throb of a motorbike can, in an instant
turn into flowers at the road side —

cauls of cellophane holding the rain.
Mothers dream of fleeing cruel kings, boys held firm
in their arms — while, on stage

the boys lose themselves in flight, up and away
wild as the wind in bare trees and the heavy curtain
falls over and over again.

Niagara

The edge is luminous, a green ribbon
of unearthly, unheavenly light lifts
and turns grey water into molten emerald
so the going-over's a fall and a tumble
through the best kind of brightness
before the long drop to the depths.

The Leaving

Today, we walked through meadows strewn
with waxy suns face-up to an unblemished sky,

passed sudden clumps of orchids then clambered
down to the cool of the disused quarry, its tumble

of granite and moss. Today, a beating heart
was stilled, someone's soul said farewell

to these fields and flowers and all things bright.
Meanwhile, skylarks sprang from new grass,

disappeared into dots, singing. We sat by the pond's
smooth water, watched the slow flapping wings

of a heron take off for a far horizon. A fish held firm
in its beak was catching the light, silver and glinting.

The Fell of Day

after Gerard Manley Hopkins

Yes, I've spent black hours fretting
but today, I slipped into my car,
drove to Port Quinn's turquoise
triangle of luminous sea, its curves

and crevices of a coast unafraid
of complexity, down lanes
that have no passing places,
(yet, we passed nevertheless)

through tunnels of flickering
mustard, bright splodges of mallow,
grass dense and smooth, lifting
like the girl's hair in the breeze.

She was mending a broken wall
in the sunshine, smiled hello.
Yes, I've tasted bitterness
and sour self-loathing
but today, I slipped into my car.

Litany for the Animals

For anteaters and ants, Abdulali's Wrinkled Frog and Abe's Salamander
Let us pray to the Lord

For all the birds of the air, buffalo that once filled the plains,
for bees and their dances, for blue butterflies of our childhoods
Let us invoke the Goddess

For cattle incarcerated in mega-dairies, for cows with udders scraping the ground,
for kind eyes of heifers and ebullience of bullocks
Let us beg for forgiveness

For dogs in their dogginess, wolves, coyotes, hyenas,
hairless Mexican dogs, dogs on the streets with the homeless,
dogs by the hearth, at our heels with hearts full of love
Let us give thanks and praise

For elephants with their graveyards and tears, tenderness
and listening feet
Let us be reverent and learn

For foxes, encroaching on cities, in dens in the woods,
for foxes, running in terror from the hounds,
for foxes, fat-brushed and burnished in the field at dawn
Let us acknowledge complexity

For the forty endangered species of Galapagos Land Snail —
bulimulus adelphus, bulimulus darwinii, bulimulus nux,
bulimulus wolfi, et cetera
Let us wonder at Gaia

For wild horses, unshod, untamed, untethered, galloping over the moor
Let us stand in admiration and awe

For horses with bit, bridle and saddle, whip, jump and stable
Let us hang our heads in shame

For the ibex, ibis, impala, iguana and iguanodon
Let us stop being an 'I' and turn into 'we'

For the jaguar alone in the empty forests of Guyana
Let us provide food and shelter

For the kangaroo, her pouch and her joey, her bounce and her boing,
for the koala beloved of children, for the kith and kin of the animals
Let us smile unto the Lord

For the lionness and ladybird, the locust and limpet, for the lark
and his joyful song
Let us sing … [sing] 'All you need is love .. All you need is love …
All you need is love, love. Love is all you need.

For the Manx cat and maned wolf, mandrill and marsh deer
Let us revere the earth our mother, and all the mothers that gave us life

For the nuthatch in the garden
Let us see the miracle of small things

For the sight of an otter sliding slick as a shadow in the shallows
of the rich river
Let us sigh an Oh! of wonder

For parakeets, parrots, peacocks, pelicans, penguins
and peregrine falcons
Let us thank the Goddess for feathered beauty in all its forms

For rabbits, their reproductive vigour, their fluffy tails and soft noses
Let us learn gentleness

For the sixty five thousand animals in danger of extinction
Let us lament them, let us say, no, no, no, no …

For Tyrannosaurus Rex and all his brothers and sisters
Let us never forget

For unicorns and six-legged antelopes, Cheshire cats and dragons
Let us pay heed to our dreams

[33]

For the Variegated Spider Monkey, Venezuelan Wood Quail,
Velvet Worm and Visayan Warty Pig
Let us honour them by knowing their names

For the whales, the dolphins, all the cetaceans roaming our oceans,
for those in captivity
Let us always choose freedom

For the thud and sudden end of extinction, for the last creature
of its kind
Mother Earth, help us make new life

For you, you, you and you,
Let us celebrate the web of creation [join hands]

For the zebra, zumbador, zebu and zho
Let us know endings are beginnings in the circle of life
and remember ant-eaters and ants, Abdulali's Wrinkled Frog
and Abe's Salamander.

Srebrenica

after the paintings by Phil Whiting

The light's unbearable
not a candle, nor an open fire
nor the glow behind curtains of home

it's an icy light

the child covers her eyes
the whiteness too bleak
the brightness too raw

if there's God in the light
where's He hiding?

we ask again
is He there?

but this light is silent —
busy with its task
of emptying the world.

Garage

There's crockery boxed for two decades,
an unfixable clock, piles
of easily replaceable books, furniture
that may or may not fit
a future home. A tatty kilim

bought when the weather
was a certain way has meaning
for a single living soul.
Someone, one day, will have no qualms
at giving all of it away.

The house holds living things
touched by the brightness of now —
but even these are destined for boxes
and garages — to be flotsam
on the seas of past love.

What will survive of us is stuff.

Walking to Rosslyn Chapel

promise of violets, loosestrife and bluebells
scent of spring ransomes as we climb to the castle

dreaming of daisies, long hours in long grass
picking daisies and counting I love yous

love you nots, weaving daisies into chains
long as the Esk in her steep rocky chasms

roses like cheeks, like lips on those faces
the flickering firelight, whisky on lips

roses like women in a hortus conclusus
books to be opened, wanton words to fly free

ungilded as lilies, naked, free in the field
not toiling like writers under the eaves

we enter the chapel under fields of bright stars
Christ raises his hand, blesses all that we are.

Beds for Writers

Tŷ Newydd, National Writers Centre for Wales

It's no surprise I should
dream so many dreams
when I sleep in beds
where so many dreamers
have slept. Their images
free as imago butterflies,
their poems, precise as
Greek pots, their stories
rising like Escher's
impossible staircases,
all invade my own word-filled
head. But, why, last night,
did the blue bus, full of people,
tip into the river? How did
I know for sure I would drown?

Forty Days and Forty Nights

i.m. Jo Durden-Smith

I called the ward — was slow to get the picture,
insisted the family were keeping vigil. It was clear
they'd be there. Do you have their number at home,
asked the nurse, they're not here. He's passed away,
she finally said. I find a buried bottle of vodka,
hunt out a photograph and look at it by candlelight.

In his London flat, his widow cannot bear the light,
sits in the darkened kitchen with his picture,
a flickering candle from the church, vodka
and black bread, reading, her voice sharp and clear,
the Russian prayers she said at his bedside, the way
he liked to hear them when they came home

to their Moscow *dacha*, where he felt most at home.
Friends often gathered there and he would light
yet another cigarette, propose a toast and sway
to his feet, welcome one and all, a tall, bearded picture
of Christian hospitality. He'd smile and clear
his throat, eloquently speak, raise high the glass of vodka.

At so many parties, he and I drank vodka.
Russia was where, once, I, too, made a home.
He went further, found a bride, fathered a clear-
eyed, clever daughter, and living lightly
moved furniture and much-loved pictures
from rented flat to house and finally right away

to London. There, he lived in the same way —
open-door, well-cooked food, wine and vodka,
his embrace always warm, always a new story. Picture
a bear-like man who knew what made a house a home.
Wife, daughter, mother-in-law know him as the light
that drew and held them. Without him, it's clear

the world's a darker place. The clouds will never clear
again. The weeks pass by. The candles burn away,
the glass is empty, the dried-out bread feels strangely light.
We prepare for the fortieth night, chill the vodka,
invite his closest friends to join us quietly at home,
ready to say goodbye to the ever-present picture.

Many waters run like love, clear as icy vodka.
Forty days have passed, he's gone, been taken home.
Sunlight floods the kitchen, illuminates his smiling picture.

The Well

after a line by Denise Levertov

They are still there and always there
the spirits of our ancestors —

fathers whispering from the ash tree
which branch is the perfect shape for the handle of an axe

They are still there and always there —
mothers teaching daughters names of flowers in the hedgerows

They are still there and always there —
faded foxgloves seeding themselves for the year after next

They are still there and always there —
pilgrims walking a grassy path to the well

saints standing in freezing water for love
cow parsley on the altar picked and offered by children

They are still there and always there —
the buried bones, white and eternal
tainting the water with life.

Cormorant

The Chinese put rings round your throat
so they can steal fish you've caught

by your own quickness. Today in the distance
your zig-zag neck and beak

become an eyelash, a black arc slipping
the grey wave.

When you're hungry, too light to dive, I read,
you swallow pebbles for weight.

Last summer, I saw five of you
make the shape of a star, drop in formation,

cutting the sea as if it were paper,
you, characters in an Oriental language,

writing of the heft of the water you part,
the cost of the fish you yield.

Wood, String, Air

Richard Durrant playing at Higher Carvedras

People wait, blanketed quiet, in the chill of evening's
coming. Strewn clouds drag their silver linings
behind us over Cornwall's almost-island mass.

He emerges between the open wings of the chapel doors,
as if born of a butterfly, in white shirt, striped trousers, bare feet.
Sits. Music starts. Air hesitates, quivers like a rabbit

in the grass before spiralling into our ears, invading our hearts
as we breathe in the fast flex of his fingers over taut string,
his hands running along the fret of our lives.

Sound weaves into early stars as we become one with Spain,
the settling moon, dispersing clouds, New York, Brazil,
the four winds busy in their spinning. The repetitive loops

thrum through wood, collide with the present and what's to come.
Minutes stretch and contract, jump through days
lost and remembered. The musician's lit up by sound until

silence, then our flat hands applauding, jolting
the air back to her emptiness. Wearing the shadow of an overcoat,
feet still bare, he fades through the chapel doors,
embraced by a butterfly.

Stone Diary

Yes, you got blood out of me alright,
lucky I don't live in a glass house.

An Olympic athlete would struggle
to throw anything as far as you are from me now.

Only the crows can imagine my surprise
when your heart grew more than cold.

Who cast the first one? Did we really turn over
every possibility? Was it so important for you to be moss-free?

You used sticks to great effect, rendered what was ours
a pile of broken bones, a soup made of water.

Two love-birds sundered with a single missile,
the ending was fixed and fired as a statue.

When we left our love behind, it wasn't just dead
and when I say I was sober, I mean, I was sober.

Squirrels

Toronto

In this city, they're black, sleek as cats
and everywhere, up trees, running
round hostas in front yards, crossing
the streets in pairs, heedless of cars,
taking what they need, knowing
that in spite of today's warmth, autumn
is falling towards them, a dark blanket
muffling their words, so now they scurry,
collecting them — *nuts, nests, shuffle*
of leaves, slow, sleep, snow, night —
long dreams of next year's seeds.

Crossing the Helford

for Penelope Shuttle and Caroline Carver

Be good, said the man to his beagle
Be quiet, said the woman to the seagull

Move, said the wind to the water
Stay, say the roses to the old wall

Walk, said my mind to my feet
Come, said the path, stop, said the fence

Remember, say the poems, remember, remember
Listen, says the wind, hearing our voices

Leave, says the boat
Let them go, says the wind, moving away

Stay, say the roses on the cottage wall
Hush, says the water to the wind

Blue, green and black says the sky to the river
and all this time, the good beagle said nothing at all.

Tree of Doors

Ancient oak tree at Trelissick ... Hen dherowenn orth Trelesik...

Centuries ago, someone's father thumbed an acorn,
still cradled in its cupule, into the yielding earth,
to be part of a Cornish hedge undulating over fields
in time to the tides below. Now, you stand alone,
trunk hollow as old bone, tip-toe on phalanges
of roots, tilting on the hillside, gateway between worlds.

When I open you, Tree of Doors, men come rushing
towards me, holy and worldly. (The secret name
of the oak tree is father). You're sacred in every forest,
grove and garden of the world, branches grasping
sky-god Jupiter, thunder-god Thor. Here, earthed Druids,
Men of Oak, love moss and damp, this milky sun and you.

Mistletoe is the divine touching your trunk, turning planks
to boats, connecting Cornwall to the sea-kingdoms
of the setting west. St Columba prays to the wind like a gull
in his oak-built chapel. St Brendan strengthens his coracle
with oak and, God-tossed by waves, conjures New Worlds.
Emperors, victorious in Rome, wear crowns of your leaves.

Like any father, you stand like a God in the field
so thunder touches you first, lightening thuds through you.
Like any daughter, I suffer too. Are they your long fingers
grasping the ground? *Bysow hir ow talhenna an dor ...*
Or my own, half-wood, half-bone? I'm thirsty for roots.
Syhes, syhes rag gwreydh. And I close you, my Tree of Doors.

Kitchen

for Tamara Jones

Five dinner plates, white with blue patterns
love their arrangement on the table

the green plate with its decoration of birds
holds the frittata blissfully

grapes, strawberries, blueberries, raspberries
have an end of summer song and sing it sweetly

cheese smoked on the Roseland is some way
from the French cheese oozing its aromas
but they both delight in being cheese

rosemary bread is prickly and oily
we need that too

someone's brought 'herring in fur coats'
gleaming beetroot, merry spring onion

at one with the 'salat iz crabov' — all claws
and cold water Northernness

oh, and there's bits of this and that
frivolous spirals of pasta, pureed apples
in floral tea cups, one saying *Mother*

it's all part of our laughter
our womanish talk, our love for each other.

Five Holy Oranges

after Anne Sexton

Evenings, they glow like bulbs
strung up for *carnaval*. A lattice
of dark leaves frames a single star.
I pull gently. Some come readily, yield

to the wrap of a hand, others resist
give way with a snap and springing
reproaches of branch. Five's perfect
when they're small, juice sharp

as street boys in the city. I rinse
each one, smooth away dust and air,
examine blemishes and insect holes,
lay them on paper on a plate, fragrant,

in the opaque light of the fridge. Tall
as a coffin, it hums all night. I dream,
naming the planets of this strange universe —
Toque, Sorriso, Boca, Lingueta, Beijo.

At dawn, I lift them like birds' eggs, tenderly.
The rest is quick, no place for mercy —
a sharpened knife, my wrists twisting
and pushing till the glass is full.

I sit in the garden's early glare,
greedily swallow the long, cool sun.

Thaw

I've been permafrost for ages,
my heart a slippery floor
for Inuit and polar bear.
Precision holes for fish
are black moons in silver
seamless winter nights.

Only an axe oiled
with steely love
can cleave me
into houses and walls,
the igloo's glisten
or an ice hotel.

If you expect me to soften —
make life easy —
you'll only have yourself to blame
for the drowning,
the unbearable blue
the shrinking floes that will hold
no one at all.

What my heart is like

after Miroslav Holub

I've never entered my heart
so all this is hearsay

when I tell of a ruby city
of cherry trees, turrets and belfries

gated by ivory bars
lifting on drumbeats.

She spoke of a palace
a Topkapi of harems and dungeons

a north room scarlet with carpets
woven by silk worms, where old loves die.

Another chamber faces south
looks out on the Marmara

floods with light from crimson water
of women giving birth to desire.

The east courtyard holds the sun.
I love it and lose it each day

to the burgundy sea. In the west
down slippery steps, cold moons

hold the hands of the world
lure fish to the surface in shimmers of silver.

I've never entered my heart
so all this is hearsay, told by a woman

who said she was wise. She went there
alone, looking for birds

but finding instead a key
that wouldn't stop bleeding, a room full of bones.

Prague

Death's always in the background
in this city where graveyards rise

to meet a low sky scarred with steeples.
The past is a castle high on a hill —

to go there, we cross sluggish water
watched by statues and sadness,

here and then gone, like my younger self
visiting a city that no longer exists,

like us, briefly, in that old hotel
on Wenceslas Square, before the something

that held us died. Yes, death's here like the rain,
dotting the river with her little black dots.

And Joy Befell Me

Some confusion as we queued at the altar,
I was suddenly ushered forward
by the pretty verger just as the priest approached.
I sank at the middle of the rail, sweet symmetry,
and as I knelt, *tout de suite*, the host arrived,
melted on my tongue, the flesh, the light,
her swinging pony tail, all the people, all as one.

Dormouse on the Bird Feeder

Small enough to slip like a shadow
through the dense fence, cradling
ink-filled eyes in the tiniest of skulls,
she was a moment of wonder held firm
in air's invisible hands and kind light
of sun, wind furrowing her tawny fur
and then was gone, borne away
on the exhalation of my brief breath.

Snapshot

The bosomy woman in a floral frock and shiny shoes
dandles her grand-daughter for somebody's camera.
The baby, head-to-toe in hand-knitted white wool,

looks astonished to be perched on the lush, curly back
of a golden retriever. The dog stares sphinx-like and, behind,
the long lawn unrolls its stripes in the sun, like bolts of silk.

Now, that land's awash with feathery grass, the dog's grave's
long-lost, along with its name and that of its owner. The woman
writing this, with untidy hair and bare feet, has no one

to record her life free from ties of children, dogs and gardens —
and wonders where such formal beauty went, finds sweet
disorder in hours sat in a kitchen alone, toying with words —

until there's a moment held firm in the afternoon light,
when she's surprised to find the posing's come right.

Lake Orta, Ten Years On

You are not champagne, nor inky Barolo
poured into my tulip-shaped glass
on the terrace of the Venus.

You are not my tears, nor espresso
in the square, served *corretto* with brandy
for my broken heart.

If I asked you your secrets
what would you say? That your shores echoed
to Georgian songs, that Nietzsche loved you too?

Do you think I don't know that like the nuns
on the island, you are *Cenerentola*
your beauty there for the taking, the Green Man

and Dragon ready to pounce. No, you are not
the Psalmist's deep waters of death,
nor the solemn tableaux on the Sacro Monte —

you're St Francis, giving bread to the birds —
a robin's impossible lightness on my open hand,
autumn leaves drifting through a woman's long hair.

If we took a boat to the Island one more time,
we could walk the Way of Silence. I'd be myself and you …
You would be everything, the words, the wind, the water.

Full Moon at Little White Alice

In spite of hats, coats and candles, we're cold and fear
is in the frosty air: for our own health, that of others,
for the planet, our families, businesses and love affairs,
paintings or projects. We're afraid of moving and changing,

the process by which butterflies leave the chrysalis,
a new-born baby first cries, tearing open her lungs.
Stagnating's not an option. Time taunts us: the ticking clock
mocking our bodies, no longer young, a slow decoupling

from our sister moon. We walk in silent meditation round
the high, granite-strewn pool, seeing, as we step with care,
a frill of thin ice form in the reeds along the edge, watch,
amazed, as Rosie suddenly sheds all of her clothes. She dives,

spine curved in a crescent, breaks the black water, sending
courage, like a scatter of stars, up into the still January air.

[*Note:* LWA is a granite-quarrying area of Cornwall]

[58]

Morning

I didn't bring my camera today,
just wanted to be in the brightness

of sea-sparkle, sky-sparkle,
light touching everything,

let my heart leap like the Dalmatian dog
jumping the waves, over and over.

The black dots of his coat
are small puddles of darkness.

He's carrying them into the water,
dousing them in diamonds of spray.